D0548811

SCANDINAVIA

A PICTURE BOOK TO REMEMBER HER BY

Designed by
DAVID GIBBON

Produced by
TED SMART

CRESCENT

INTRODUCTION

Situated in the north-west of Europe is the unspoiled region of Scandinavia. It is composed of the countries of Norway, Sweden, Denmark and Finland but also includes Greenland, an Arctic island larger than Australia, which is a province of Denmark. As a unit these countries have a great deal in common and yet each is a fascinatingly individual land in its own right.

The hardy yet carefree people of Norway are dominated by their high mountains and the sea that stretches along one thousand miles of rugged coastline. The majestic mountains divide the land and isolate small villages whose inhabitants struggle to eke a living from the barren slopes. It is to the sea, therefore, that many Norwegians turn for their livelihood and their fishing industry is all important.

For the tourist, Norway is a wonderful country. There is the breathtaking beauty of the fjords, the challenge of the mountains (where thousand-foot high rock faces wait to be climbed), sparkling streams to be fished for salmon and trout and winter sports centres that are the equal of any to be found in the rest of Europe. In addition waterfalls, lakes, glaciers and grottoes combine to make up some of the most spectacular scenery in the world. A journey to the North Cape, a craggy granite cliff, is unforgettable. People make the journey for the unique experience of viewing the Midnight Sun, as Norway has more hours of daylight in summer than any inhabited country in the world.

In its own lovely setting stands the bright and hospitable city of Oslo, a prosperous sea port and the capital of Norway. Here may be seen some of the famous ships that were used by the Vikings, the so-called "sea-warriors" of Scandinavia. These ships, strongly constructed of oak and lashed together with whale bristle, were used by the Vikings for trade and exploration as well as for plundering and terrorizing large parts of Western Europe.

Much of Danish history is linked with the Vikings, for, although Denmark is the smallest of the Scandinavian countries, she at one time ruled the whole of Norway and Sweden, parts of Germany and most of England. The Danes are a very cosmopolitan race and Copenhagen is considered by many to be one of the most delightful capitals in the world. Situated on Zealand, an island that is just as flat as the rest of Denmark, the city has much of interest to offer the visitor. The Tivoli Gardens with its fountains, orchestras, theatres, lakes and restaurants provide entertainment for all tastes. Sitting on her rock and looking out to sea, the statue of The Little Mermaid is as famous a landmark of Denmark as the Sphinx is of Egypt, and the Langelinie Promenade on which the mermaid rests is a favourite strolling place.

To the west of Copenhagen, on the island of Funen, is Odense, a city made famous as the birthplace of Hans Christian Anderson, who was probably the most gifted writer of fairy tales the world has known. In addition to its association with the writer, Funen also offers the visitor beautiful landscape and a wealth of medieval castles and manor houses.

Lovers of William Shakespeare find Elsinore, on the north-east coast of Denmark, a great attraction, for Kronborg Castle, a fascinating renaissance building, was used as the setting for Hamlet.

Although lacking the rugged splendour of the other Scandinavian countries, Denmark has the advantage of rich farmland which makes possible the production of fine cheeses, butter and bacon. Danish cuisine is very appetizing, particularly the open sandwich called Smørrebrød which is served throughout Scandinavia.

Sweden is the largest country in the Scandinavian peninsula. It is a land of great forests and thousands of lakes, of sophisticated towns and cities in the south and simple lumberjack camps in the north. The imposing capital, Stockholm, was originally founded on one small island, where Lake Mälar reaches the Baltic Sea, but it gradually spread to other islands and finally to the mainland, to become a city. Stockholm is known as the 'Venice of the North' and, as planning is strictly controlled, it remains a city of beautiful palaces and imaginative modern buildings with many parks and tree-lined squares. It also contains one of the narrowest thoroughfares in the world, the so-called 'Yard-wide Lane'.

One of Stockholm's most distinguished citizens was Alfred Nobel, a Swedish chemist, who invented dynamite and a smokeless gunpowder. He amassed a vast fortune, the bulk of which he left in the form of a trust for the endowment of five awards known as Nobel Prizes. These prizes are awarded annually to people who have made important discoveries in, or contributions to, chemistry, physics, medicine, literature and peace.

Across the Gulf of Bothnia lies Finland, or Suomi as the Finns call their country. Finland was part of the Kingdom of Sweden for six hundred years but, early in the 18th century, Sweden and Russia disputed possession and in 1809 Finland became a Grand Duchy of Russia. After the Russian revolution of 1917, however, Finland declared itself an independent republic and today, although still geographically isolated, the country is politically allied to Scandinavia.

Finland is possibly the most unspoiled of all the four countries that make up Scandinavia and her beauty is immortalized in the music of the composer Sibelius. Like Sweden, Finland has a myriad of lakes and, along the western and southern coasts, an archipelago of 30,000 islands which provides sheltered waters and unrivalled sailing.

Helsinki, the capital, lies on the south coast of Finland and it is an important port although its natural harbour has to be kept open by ice-breakers during the winter. The city has many fine buildings, including a superb stadium which was built when Helsinki was host to the Olympic Games in 1952.

Lapland is a region that includes Northern Scandinavia and part of Russia. It extends from the Norwegian coast to the White Sea. Lapland lies within the Arctic Circle and it is a cold, white wilderness in winter, with three months of continuous darkness, and a fierce, colourful land in summer when it enjoys three months of continuous daylight. The highly cultured Lapps, many of whom speak three or four languages, are dependent on their large herds of reindeer for food, transport and clothing. Wherever the reindeer roam, so do the nomadic Lapps and it is vital to the continued existence of the 30,000 Lapps who are left that they remain free to wander, paying little heed to frontiers.

The Lapps are, perhaps, the most colourful people in this part of the world but, in spite of their different customs and languages, all the Scandinavian people have a profound awareness of their surroundings and a strong conviction that they must preserve their beautiful countries.

Left: Nordfjord, Stryn, Norway.

DENMARK

Copenhagen, Denmark's capital, was first mentioned in written records in 1043 but it has traces of habitation that go back many thousands of years before that. The remains of the first fortress, built to protect the small town in 1167, may be seen today in the cellars of Christiansborg Palace. The palace was unfortunately destroyed by fire and the royal residence was transferred to the Amalienborg Palace. Christiansborg was subsequently rebuilt on the original site and the present palace was erected between 1907 and 1928.

Every day, at noon, the Changing of the Guard takes place *top left* at Amalienborg Palace and when the Queen is in residence the guards march through the city behind their band.

In addition to being used commercially, Christianshaven Canal *centre left* is popular with visitors, who can enjoy frequent and extensive trips along the city's waterways.

Copenhagen has a wealth of museums. The open-air Museum *right* is part of the National Museum and consists of old farm buildings and houses reconstructed and furnished as in former days.

The Tivoli Gardens are undoubtedly one of Copenhagen's great attractions, certainly to the many thousands of visitors who come to the city each year. This world famous amusement park was laid out on the site of the city walls in 1843. Flowers and fountains, open-air performances of plays and ballet, amusements and restaurants: there is something for everyone in Tivoli. Although the gardens are fresh, green and attractive by day, it is at night that 100,000 lights turn the place into a fairyland as the pictures *above* and *right* show.

Pictured *left* is Copenhagen's yacht harbour.

A symbol of Copenhagen instantly recognized throughout the world is the statue of the 'Little Mermaid' *overleaf*.

Just 22 miles north of Copenhagen, at Hillerød, stands Frederiksborg Castle, *above* Denmark's Museum of National History, with the Palace Chapel which contains an organ dating from 1612.

Udergaard Castle, *above right* near Flavenskjold, Jutland.

The Gatehouse of Valdemarslot Castle at Taasinge, Funen *right*.

Denmark is fortunate in having not only fine agricultural and grazing land which is instrumental in making her world famous for her dairy produce, but also in possessing a very extensive coastline and many natural harbours, both essential to her fishing industry. Hvide Sande *below left* is one such fishing village, situated on a narrow isthmus on the west coast of Jutland.

Gavnø manor house *left* was originally a convent and was founded in 1400 by Queen Margarethe I. It is situated in south Zealand, about 85km. from Copenhagen.

Engelsholm Castle *below* is on the east coast of Jutland, near the old town of Vejle.

The Faeroes are in the North Atlantic ocean. The group comprises eighteen islands, seventeen of which are inhabited. Sandoy *overleaf* is one of the islands in this group.

NORWAY

Oslo is Norway's bright and open capital city. It is also a major port, not only for commercial shipping and cruise liners thronging the harbour *centre left,* but also for fishing vessels. Oslo's maritime tradition is further reinforced by the Norwegian Maritime Museum's fascinating collection of boats and ships. Of outstanding interest is the Viking Ship Museum at Bygdøy.

The City Hall *top left* is of great interest to visitors as it is richly endowed with paintings and sculptures by leading Norwegian artists.

As with any major city, Oslo has all the amenities that may be expected, such as shops, hotels, restaurants and parks, as well as a university and a Royal Palace. The palace stands in the Slottsparken, at the western end of Karl Johans Gate *bottom left.*

Akershus Castle *right* was built in about 1300 by Haakon V Magnusson, the last of the kings of Harald's lineage. A fire in 1527 caused extensive damage and it was rebuilt by Christian IV between 1588 and 1648. It has been considerably restored, and the castle halls are now used by the Norwegian government on ceremonial occasions.

There are very few places in Norway –
and certainly none in the rest of
Europe – where the landscape is so
richly endowed with the mountains,
waterfalls and fjords that are to be
found in the Romsdal area *left*.

A fjord is simply a huge cleft in the
mountains, into which the waters of
the ocean have poured. They reach
like long, blue fingers deep into the
countryside. The mountains tower
above the waters and cast their
reflections into them as at Stryn *top
right*, creating some of the most
majestic and beautiful landscapes to
be seen anywhere in the world.

In a clearing in the trees stands the
hut *below* where some of the lovely
music of Grieg was composed.

Some distance inland from the ocean,
but still very much in 'fjord country',
farm animals graze the pastures at
Oldedalan *centre right* and at
Geiranger *bottom right*.

Bergen is Norway's second city and a major international port. It lies in the heart of the fjord country, overlooked by seven hills. As the pictures on these pages and *overleaf* show, the harbour area provides the most picturesque of Bergen's many attractions but everywhere the happy relationships between the old and the new is a delight to the visitor.

Modern skiing began in Norway. It spread all over the world to become, eventually, the enormously popular winter sport that it is today

Winter in Norway is a paradise for the winter sports enthusiast. It is not necessary, however, to be a devotee of sport to appreciate the beauty of the snow-laden landscape as at Telemark *right*.

It might reasonably be supposed that northern Norway, lying as it does within the Arctic Circle, would be a land sheathed in ice. Thanks to the Gulf Stream, however, this is not the case and, whilst the winters can be very cold indeed, summer can provide surprisingly warm, even hot, days when it is a delight to walk in the open country, breathing the fresh, clear air and enjoy a little fishing in one of the many streams and rivers as at Otertind *far left*, or Aldasnes in Romsdal, which lies much farther south, *left*.

Kvinesdal *above* is about as far from the Arctic Circle as it is possible to be in Norway. It lies between Stavanger and Kristiansand, not far from the seafaring town of Mandal, on the south coast of the country.

Vik *top right* is a small farming and fishing community that lies on the banks of the Sogn fjord.

Stave churches are a unique feature of the Norwegian countryside and many of them have survived for hundreds of years. The church of Eidsborg in Telemark *centre right* is typical. This particular example was built in the 13th century.

Norway is rich in forests and a great number of the buildings are constructed of wood as these log cabins at Skridulaupen *bottom right* illustrate.

At the mouth of the Geiranger fjord *left* lies Ålesund, Norway's largest and most important fishing town. Its setting is ideal, with the sea in front and the beautiful Sunnmøre Alps as a background. Among Ålesund's more notable sights is the medieval Borgund church and an open-air museum.

There is something for practically everyone in Norway. The changing seasons, of course, provide different views of even the same landscapes and smaller, subtler changes from day to day can transform a sparkling, brilliant scene into one of soft, mysterious romanticism *below*.

Tromsø *above right* is the largest
town, in area, in the whole of Norway.
Here is to be found the most northern
university in the world, and a
mountain cable car offering, at its
highest point, quite breathtaking
views, and an Arctic Ocean Cathedral.

Narvik *right* is superbly situated on
a peninsula with, to the south, the Beis
fjord and the Rombaks fjord to the
north. In terms of tonnage Narvik is
one of the world's major export
harbours, based on the storage and
shipment of iron-ore from the mines
of Sweden. It is also a centre for alpine
sports and offers a wide range of
facilities for such pursuits. The
Midnight Sun is visible at Narvik from
the end of May to the middle of July.

The Lofoten Islands are a group of
islands off the north-west coast of
Norway. Reine *left* lies at the very tip
of the Lofotens and hardly anywhere
in the world are there such graceful
peaks, linked together by such
razorsharp ridges.

Kirkehamn *above* is a so-called
'out-port' lying at the entrance to Lista
fjord, on the south coast of Norway.

The awe-inspiring magnificence of
Geiranger fjord is shown to advantage
overleaf.

Hammerfest *left* is on the north coast of Norway, well within the Arctic Circle, and it is, in fact, the most northerly town in the world. Despite this, fishing excursions are regularly arranged for tourists.

A wooden stave church *below* at Borgund and a picturesque setting for a church *left centre* at Jlster.

Skjernøisund *left* is on the southern coast of Norway, near Mandal. On this coast the most famous beach in the country is to be found, at Sjøsanden.

Following the great curve of the southern coast past Kristiansand brings the visitor to Risør *above right*, facing onto the Skagerrak. Continuing the journey would lead directly into the Oslo fjord with the harbour of Drøbak *right* on the right bank before finally reaching Oslo.

SWEDEN

Sweden's capital, Stockholm, lies between lake Mälaren and the Baltic Sea. It is widely considered to be not only one of the most beautiful capital cities in the world but also the cleanest. Stockholm was founded in the 13th century on an island and, in much the same way as its neighbouring capital, Copenhagen, it gradually spread, first to other, nearby, islands and then to the mainland. It is a city of contrasts, retaining all the charm of an earlier age whilst at the same time it has all the trappings of the modern commercial city that it is. There are no less than fifty-two museums, five hundred restaurants and cafés, ample hotel accommodation, lively night entertainment and it is even possible to swim and fish in the centre of the city! Many people who work in the city and live outside it travel to work by boat during the summer months, and it is not difficult to see why Stockholm is called "the Venice of the North".

Left and below are two general views of the city of Stockholm and the pictures *top right and centre right* show the Royal Palace.

The Grand Hotel is pictured *bottom right* with the Strom Bridge in the foreground.

Overleaf: Kornhamnstorg to the south of the Royal Palace.

Gamla Stan is the Old Town of Stockholm *centre right*. It is a romantic quarter of narrow, cobblestone streets, restaurants and antique shops.

Sergels Torg by night *below* and by day *bottom right*. The Grand Hotel and Strombron *right*.

Riddarholm Church *left* was built in the 13th century and is the final resting place of many of Sweden's kings and queens.

Mariefred, Södermanland, *overleaf* is a popular site for campers.

Oland *left* is an island in the Baltic Sea off the east coast of Sweden. It is separated from the mainland by the Kalmarsund, and it was often the scene of fierce battles during the Northern wars.

All over the world autumn is a season that transforms and beautifies. The yellows, golds and reds that appear at this time add colour to a landscape that will be barren until the return of spring. The lovely views *right, below and below right* were all taken in Skog, on the east coast of Sweden.

Lysekil *overleaf* is on the west coast of Sweden where the waters of the Skagerrak flow inland to form the Gullmaren fjord.

The harbour at Strangnas is pictured *above*. It stands on the shore of a lake that is dotted with many small islands, rather like an inland sea.

Log cabins *left* at the lakeside at Hjarpesto.

It was at Kalmar *below* that the Union of Kalmar was formed in 1397, uniting Sweden, Norway and Denmark into a single monarchy that lasted until 1523.

Gothenburg is the heart, and capital, of Sweden's west coast. It is a delightful city of parks, wide streets, excellent shops, museums and art galleries. *Top and centre right* are two views of the statue of Poseidon and Gothenberg's harbour is shown *bottom right*.

The bridge *left* linking the mainland with Oland Island is, at 6,070 metres, the longest bridge in Europe. Work on the bridge started in January 1968 and it was opened to the general public in September 1972.

The lighthouse *below* stands on a rocky promontory on Sweden's east coast, guiding shipping in the Gulf of Bothnia, such as the fishing boats, *bottom*.

Sweden is a land of rivers and lakes *right*, which provide, for the visitor, not only idyllic scenery but also an abundance of outdoor activities.

FINLAND

Finland is a land of thousands of lakes and miles of coastline. It has a temperate climate due to the vicinity of the Atlantic Ocean and the Gulf Stream.

Helsinki, Finland's capital, lies on the southern coast, on the shores of the Gulf of Finland. It is a modern city, unlike many of Europe's older capitals, and yet it is not a brash city. There are areas that give a genuine picture of the architecture and atmosphere of the past.

As with most of Scandinavia's cities and towns water has played an important part in Helsinki's development, and indeed it still does. The Zoological Gardens, for instance, are situated on an island which is reached by ferry, surely a unique situation! Finland is justly famous for the quality of its glassware, ceramics, textiles, fashion and jewellery, all of which may be purchased in Helsinki's excellent shopping centres.

Left: Helsinki's cathedral.

Helsinki's City Theatre is shown *right*, and *below and overleaf* are two views of the city from the harbour.

Olavinlinna Castle in Savonlinna *right* is the best-preserved medieval castle in Scandinavia. It is a popular tourist attraction, is the setting for festivals and has a unique congress centre. Much of the castle, including the King's Hall, has been restored since 1961. The international opera festival, which is held every year at the end of July and beginning of August, dates from 1967. The town of Savonlinna is in East Savo province which offers the visitor the most extensive lake scenery in Europe.

Tammisaari Castle *below* is situated on the coast of the Gulf of Finland, west of Helsinki.

The University and University Library *top left* in Senate Square, Helsinki.

A view *centre left* of the skyline of Helsinki.

As befits a modern country, Finland has an extensive railway network. The picture *bottom left* shows a section of the system in Helsinki.

Turku *left* is the former capital of Finland and has a prominent place in Northern history. Rather than being founded it developed naturally at the crossing of the northern trade routes. The magnificent historic monuments to be seen there are unique in Finland.

At Kerimaki *right* stands the largest stave, or wooden, church in the world.

Haymaking *below* near Savonlinna.

The second oldest town in Finland is Porvoo *centre left and left*, about thirty miles from Helsinki. Porvoo has always been a home for poets, authors and artists and it remains so to this day. The old town is, undoubtedly, a great attraction for visitors to Porvoo. The original town dates back to the middle ages and although wars and fires have destroyed it many times it has always been rebuilt. Many of the houses surrounding the cathedral, which was built in the early part of the 15th century, date from the 1700's.

The picture *overleaf* epitomises the beauty of the landscape of Finland.

Lapland is a region of Northern
Scandinavia and the Lapps are a
largely nomadic people, being
dependent for their livelihood on the
huge herds of reindeer that roam the
area. They are a colourful, cultivated
and highly intelligent race who now
number only some 30,000.

Lapland is a wild region of forests
and fells but, thanks to Finland's
excellent system of communications,
it is within easy reach of the rest of the
country and offers facilities and
services that are of the same high
standard as those in other parts of
Finland.

First published in Great Britain 1978 by Colour Library International Ltd.
© Illustrations: CLI/Bruce Coleman Ltd. Colour separations by La Cromolito, Milan, Italy.
Display and text filmsetting by Focus Photoset, London, England.
Printed and bound by Group Poligrafici Calderara - Bologna - Italy
Published by Crescent Books, a division of Crown Publishers Inc.
All rights reserved.
Library of Congress Catalogue Card No. 77-18459
CRESCENT 1978